C000128443

BEDFORD

RICHARD WILDMAN

The
History
Press

For Dorothy Wildman

Men of the 9th Argyll & Sutherland Highlanders on the march along The Embankment early in the First World War. Nearest the camera is the Town and County Club (built 1885, demolished 1971), with the Swan Hotel in the background.

First published in 1995
This edition published 2009

The History Press
The Mill, Brimscombe Port
Stroud, Gloucestershire, GL5 2QG
www.thehistorypress.co.uk

British Library Cataloguing in Publication Data.
A catalogue record for this book is available from the British Library.

ISBN: 978 0 7524 5321 7

Typesetting and origination by The History Press
Printed in Great Britain

Contents

This photograph was taken as evidence of the existence of ancient lights on a site in Howard Street, where Howard Chambers would soon replace this brick and timber barn in 1893. The old walls on the right still stand at the rear of properties in Mill Street.

Introduction

This is my fifth book of photographs of old Bedford since 1974, and it may be appropriate to offer some thoughts on how the appreciation of old photographs can illuminate for us the legacy of past building and the daily life it encompassed.

Certain people have always collected historic photographs, sometimes as evidence of property boundaries or ancient lights, and sometimes as works of art. Some early photographers believed their new medium would replace painting itself and often composed landscape, architectural and portrait views accordingly. However, it was soon realised that the artist's living eye could always produce an image of at least equal value to the literal and undiscriminating record of the camera. Works by the painters Edward Hull and Bradford Rudge are included here because their impressions of places such as St Peter's Green and St Mary's Street in the early years of photography are much more informative than any comparable photograph, the first of which to survive dates from several years later. The pencil draughtsman A.G. Glass produced sketches with a vibrancy of detail beyond the ability or selective criteria of many painters, and they recall the vigour of the unknown artist who drew John Bunyan preaching outside the otherwise unrecorded medieval Guildhall in the 1650s. (No one ever recorded – as far as is known – Bunyan's prison, which was the county gaol on the corner of Silver Street and High Street: various views of the town gaol on the old bridge were published instead). A watercolour by Thomas Fisher is one of only two representations of the Sessions House in St Paul's Square, and I have included it to show its family resemblance to the former Grammar School (now the Old Town Hall) which stands nearby.

The County Record Office (now Bedfordshire and Luton Archives and Records Service) is the main repository of historic Bedford photographs (and other forms of illustration), although good collections also exist in the Central Library and Bedford Museum. Despite the use already made of its resources, the record office collection still contains a wealth of unpublished or little-known photographs, many of which were given or lent for copying by local people. The County Council and its departments have also caused photographs to be taken specially, often in case of threatened demolition or alteration of landmarks. Some of these pictures are in this book, for example the Union Street cottages and Howard House and its neighbours, which were in danger of demolition in the 1970s.

It has been particularly pleasing to include sequences of photographs taken of Midland Road station before it was demolished in 1978: this was an example of railway architecture begun in 1859 and scarcely altered after 1868. The building of the Bedford Modern School quad in 1906–08 was recorded by Alfred Burns, the school secretary and an enthusiastic amateur photographer. The first two pictures appeared in the school magazine *The Eagle* at the time, but the contrasting views of the old Harpur Hospital and the quad under construction could not have been published until after his collection came to light in the late 1970s.

Bedford grew because of the expansion of the Harpur Trust schools in the late nineteenth century, the only heavy industry at that time being the manufacture of Howard ploughs at Britannia Works. The great increase in residential development, especially of large Victorian houses (though none quite so large as Holbrook in De Parys Avenue) and their only slightly smaller Edwardian successors, is the result of this important phase in Bedford's history. Here I can speak of links with the past, as I was taught by Molly Evans, daughter of the Rev. H.W. Evans who built 9 Dynevor Road, and learned much from Ralph Conisbee, whose father Albert, a builder, was in business with Albert Prosser around the turn of the century. Dr Hervey Wyatt, the last private owner of Austin Canons, whom I met shortly before his death in 1977, told me he was introduced as a small boy to George Hurst, who built 75 High Street (later Dust's) in 1851.

The centenary is approaching of the demolition by Bedford Corporation of the Friary Farm in 1899, to make way for a recreation ground, which was itself largely swallowed up in road-widening over thirty years ago. As these words are being written, Bedford Borough Council is seriously contemplating cutting down the middle four 120-year-old lime trees (see p. 32, bottom) in front of the retained and restored Blore façade of the former Bedford Modern School in Harpur Street. Ironically the same justification is being employed now, as nearly a century ago: more space for public recreation, only this time not swings and roundabouts but whirligigs and a permanent podium. Those who do not learn from history are indeed condemned to repeat past mistakes. The middle four lime trees were cut down in January 1995.

Many of the accepted features of daily life in post-war Bedford (as elsewhere) have now disappeared, as public tastes and economic conditions have changed. The County Theatre (attendance at pantomimes there is still a vivid memory) closed in 1960 after a long decline, though the auditorium (without its Edwardian decor, removed in 1957) remains almost intact. It is now Mount Zion Pentecostal Church. The big old cinemas have vanished more completely than any single specimen of building since the dissolution of the monasteries. Churches and chapels have closed, but some suitable uses have been found, as with Holy Trinity (though not St Leonard's). Even the *Bedfordshire Times* ceased separate publication on 21 April 1995, in its 150th anniversary year. All of us are witnesses to change, some aspects of which are inevitable, others less so, and old photographs make it possible for visual memories to outlast the span of many lifetimes.

Richard Wildman, 1995 and 2009

OLD BEDFORD

The Rev. Charles Farrar (see p. 11, bottom) claimed that 42–44 High Street (seen here c. 1960) had been the town's Market House, which Patricia Bell has proved stood in the middle of the High Street from about 1680 to 1791. The three first-floor oriel windows could have come from the Market House. The central window was saved for Bedford Museum by its director F.W. Kuhlicke when 42–44 High Street was demolished in 1964, but is no longer in the collection.

This pencil sketch of St Peter's Green was drawn by Bradford Rudge (1813–85), drawing master at the Grammar School, probably *c.* 1840. The ancient church of St Peter de Merton is flanked by Bury Farm (left) and the rectory (right).

This watercolour of 1858 by Edward Hull (1823–1906) shows St Peter's Green looking in the opposite direction. The first two old houses (from left) were the Stone House in The Broadway (demolished 1936) and no. 10 (demolished *c.* 1932, see p. 48, top). Bury Farm (with gables) was demolished in 1881 to make the approach to De Parys Avenue.

Looking south down St Mary's Street, *c.* 1850, in a watercolour attributed to Bradford Rudge. Apart from St Mary's Church (left) and St John's Church (in the distance), the sole surviving structure on the east side is the King's Arms (left of large tree). The west side of the street was mostly demolished in the 1960s and '70s. The clump of small trees (right) stood on St Mary's Square.

This postcard view of St Mary's Street, sold by A.T. Covington at no. 19, is postmarked 28 September 1907. The corner property (now College House) still stands on the west side (left). All the buildings shown here on the east side still stand, with the King's Arms (right) being easily identifiable with Rudge's picture.

The Friary Farm, seen from the east side, *c*. 1890, incorporated remains of the cloister of the Grey Friars (dissolved in 1538). In 1898 Bedford Corporation resolved to demolish the building to provide a recreation ground. Only the mayor, George Wells, and Alderman William Roff voted against. It was the ominous beginning to a century of destruction of Bedford's historic past.

The Priory Street recreation ground on the site of the Friary Farm, *c*. 1903. The caption to the Buck brothers' print of the Grey Friars (published in 1730) referred instead to Newnham Priory, hence the inaccurate naming of Priory Street. In the background are Beauchamp Row (right) and the Priory Street bowling green (see p. 64, bottom).

The worst loss of a part of Bedford's architectural heritage in the inter-war period was that of the Old George Inn, off the west side of High Street, seen here in an early nineteenth-century drawing by A.K. Burkitt. The fifteenth-century inn may have incorporated earlier masonry. A carving of St George and the dragon stood in a niche (left of archway).

The Rev. Charles Farrar, author of *Old Bedford* (1926), identified the Old George as the Prioratus or town house of the prior of Newnham, rather than (what is more likely) the town's principal inn, owned by the priory. After his death in 1931 a committee tried to secure the building's preservation in his memory, erecting the plaque shown left. The upper part of the Old George was destroyed in 1937; the inner north face of the archway (centre), though not the arch itself, still survives behind Debenhams.

Described by Sir Nikolaus Pevsner as 'the only Georgian public building of interest in the county', the Old Town Hall is the former Grammar School, endowed by Sir William Harpur and Dame Alice, his wife, in 1566. The statue of Harpur in contemporary (i.e. Georgian) dress was added when the building was refronted in 1767. The Grammar School moved to the present Bedford School site in 1892.

The Sessions House in St Paul's Square, which was built in 1753 and replaced by the Shire Hall in 1881, bears some resemblance to the Grammar School nearby. The watercolour is by Thomas Fisher, c. 1820; no photograph is known to exist.

Section Two

ALONG THE

MAIN LINE

James and Frederick Howard, sons of John Howard the ironfounder, opened Britannia Works in

Kempston Road in 1859 as a manufactory of steel ploughs. General Garibaldi, the Italian

liberator, visited the works on 15 April 1864. His party has alighted from the train (right) on

the main line from Hitchin. Garibaldi left Bedford at 3.15 p.m., his four-hour tour having

included James Howard's Clapham Park Farm, where he saw steam ploughs in action.

Midland Road station was opened in 1859 and enlarged in 1868. This shows the main entrance and *porte-cochère* from the south. The station was demolished in 1978, following the opening of the new Midland station on a new site to the north, and was replaced by W.H. Smith's Do-It-All store.

The main concourse looking towards the entrance, across the site of the original track-bed of the line to Hitchin (covered over at this point in 1868, when the main line to St Pancras was opened).

View from the north, showing the site of the original track-bed (left) and the canopies of 1859, linked together to enlarge the passenger concourse in 1868.

The main line looking towards the northern footbridge, transferred to Bedford from another station in the 1930s.

This rare print, apparently a letterhead, shows a projected mid-1860s development by the architect John Usher on the west side of Ashburnham Road. The centre pair were no. 32 (Ellerslie) and no. 34 (Shenstone Lodge), but on the left no. 30 (The Elms) was built to a different design, and the house on the right was never built. The sites were cleared in about 1975 for the new station car-park.

The Territorial Army headquarters, seen here in 1977, was built in Ashburnham Road in 1912, architect J.H. Fenning, on the site of a farmhouse called Woodcroft. The HQ was demolished in the mid-1980s after the removal of the TA to the Kempston Barracks site, and was replaced by Braemar Court flats.

BEDFORD AT WAR

A mounted escort of Imperial Yeomanry during the visit of the Boer War hero General Sir

John French, leaving Midland Road station yard on 24 July 1902. General French,

whose sister-in-law Mrs Thornton lived at 21 Kimbolton Road, received the freedom of

the borough on 9 October the same year.

The mounted escort proceeds eastwards along Midland Road past the corner of Gwyn Street (left).

The skirl of the pipes was often heard in Bedford Park and streets during the Highland Division's sojourn in the town, from the outbreak of the First World War in August 1914 until the following spring.

Highlanders on the march at the eastern entrance to Bedford Park. Most of the troops were encamped in tents in the park, but some were billeted in private houses or empty property.

Highlanders stand easy in The Grove, with the side of 19a Goldington Road (now replaced by Graylaw House), left, and 4 Goldington Road (now offices) in the background.

Soldiers of the 6th Gordon Highlanders assemble in Harpur Street in front of the ivy-clad Blore façade. In the background are Murdoch's music shop and the White Horse public house (site of Marks & Spencer).

St Cuthbert's Church (built in 1847, with later enlargements) overlooks a detachment of 9th Argyll & Sutherland Highlanders moving north up St Cuthbert's Street, with Brumwell (later Banks), fruiterer, at no. 2 (right), demolished in 1984. The man with the bicycle is said to be George Armstrong, the butcher.

This photograph of Highlanders marching south from the Town Bridge was taken by Drake Sadler in 1915. The commercial premises at 2 and 4 St Mary's Street, once private residences of Ouse Navigation merchants, were demolished in 1964 and 1972 respectively.

Bedfordians assemble to read the casualty lists posted outside the *Bedfordshire Times* office at 22 Mill Street, demolished in 1972, and now the site of *Bedfordshire on Sunday*. A corner of no. 20 (McConnells, house agent) appears at left.

If this photograph *does* show Armistice Day in Bedford in 1922, the public attendance appears to be small. The reason may be that the memorial on The Embankment (which is out of the picture to the right and shows a figure of justice armed, designed by C.S. Jagger) had already been unveiled on 20 July that year by the Lord Lieutenant, S.H. Whitbread (far right).

Joe Clough (1886–1977), once described as the dean of Bedford's immigrant community, came to England from Jamaica in 1906. An ambulance driver in France in the First World War, he moved to Bedford in 1919 to drive buses and later a taxi. He is shown collecting for the Earl Haig Poppy Fund outside 3 The Embankment (present site of the Christie Almshouses).

The use of a Bren gun as an anti-aircraft weapon being demonstrated at a Territorial Army recruiting display on the forecourt of the Swan Hotel, 25 April 1939.

On the outbreak of war in September 1939, 13,000 women and children were evacuated from London to Bedford. Children allocated to homes in the villages are seen here assembling at the canteen on the fairground site opposite the Electricity Works before being taken to their billets by bus.

ARP wardens' post being constructed on the Bank Buildings site in 1940. On the right is the side of 1 St Paul's Square, former town house of the Barnard family of bankers, with their stable block (demolished in about 1977) at the rear.

The wreckage of a Bell Aerocobra plane which crashed into back-yards in Greyfriars Walk, narrowly missing the Roise Street Sunday School, on the afternoon of Sunday 19 October 1941. Pilot Officer Peter Hewitt, who had left Bedford School the previous year, was killed instantly.

Home Guard parade along High Street, March 1942. Lloyds Bank and Charnley's, with its distinctive spectacle sign, are now empty. Phoenix Chambers (1928) was cleaned and Arthur Day (costumier) closed down, both in 1995; Belfast Linen is now High Street Dental Practice.

Workers from W.H. Allen's crossing Ford End Road railway bridge after the air-raid on 23 July 1942. On the right is the County Theatre (with flagpole) and its damaged canopy.

The ruins of the Assembly Ballroom being demolished after the air-raid. The site remained vacant until 1952, when the Court School of Dancing was built, later to become part of the bingo club which occupied the former theatre next door from 1962 until it closed on 13 August 1995. It is now Mount Zion Pentecostal Church.

Half of the Grosvenor Hotel at 5–7 Ashburnham Road was also destroyed in the raid. The site of no. 5 later accommodated the pre-fab hut known as the Grosvenor Centre. The former Queen's Hotel is now Stephen Ross House (flats).

The Castle Ward ARP wardens parade south down High Street at the end of the war. The optician Deryck Humphriss (at no. 15) later emigrated to the town of Benoni in Natal, founded by Sir George Farrar, a grandson of John Howard the ironfounder.

Impromptu celebrations of the end of the war, seen from the Bank Buildings site, 1945. Murkett's (left) was formerly the George Inn (present site of Swan Court).

Street party in Greyfriars Walk to celebrate VE Day, 8 May 1945. In the background is the chimney of the Muntona malt extract factory (previously Jarvis's brewery). Everything here was swept away by redevelopment in the early 1960s. The high-pressure water-main was to assist the fire brigade in case of an incendiary attack.

BEDFORD MODERN
SCHOOL

Demolition of all Bedford Modern School buildings behind the Blore tower and façade
(right) took place in mid-1974, following the school's move to Manton Lane. Most of
the quad has already gone, and the art room and former physics laboratories (centre) are
fast disappearing. The site is now occupied by the Harpur (shopping) Centre.

This remarkable series of photographs, taken by Alfred Burns, secretary of Bedford Modern School, shows the rebuilding of the area known as the quad (quadrangle), formerly the site of the Harpur Hospital, between 1906 and 1908. Here, the Rev. P.G. Langdon crosses from the adapted buildings of the Hospital (an orphanage which closed in 1871) to the school workshops, converted from the hospital kitchens. In the background is the Blore tower, built in 1833.

Now we see the view in the opposite direction, again with 'Piggy' Langdon (later to be curator of the school museum) and 'Joey' Church, the school carpenter, but now including the fives courts. The centre gable belongs to the Harpur Girls' Elementary School further west.

Looking south from the Midland Road side of the quad. Left (with pair of first-floor windows) is the Prichard Museum (1886); in the centre are the former Harpur Hospital outbuildings, with the Blore tower beyond; to the right are the cloisters with science laboratories above (1895).

The hospital buildings have now gone, except for the section (right) which contained the school lavatories. New classrooms stand to the right of the tower, and the gymnasium (converted into the school hall in 1929) and an adjoining two-storey classroom block are under construction.

A familiar sight to the post-war generations of Bedford Modern School pupils: the staircase of the Liberal Club in Midland Road (see p. 35, bottom), whose large upper room was rented by the Harpur Trust as an extra classroom.

The east side of Harpur Street, *c.* 1903, showing (left) St Paul's Wesleyan Sunday Schools of 1883 (demolished in 1969) and the portico of the General Library, now the Harpur Suite. On the right are the railings of Bedford Modern School and the lime trees, four of which were cut down in 1995.

Section Five

COMMERCE AND INDUSTRY

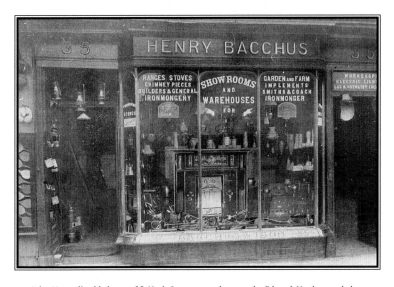

John Howard's old shop at 35 High Street was taken over by Edward Moulton and then Henry Bacchus (shown here c. 1903). Frederic Gale Ltd acquired Bacchus in about 1950. In 1969 they sold out to Gibbs & Dandy of Luton, who closed down these premises ten years later (see also p. 44, top).

This photograph, taken at the election of Sir Arthur Black as Liberal MP for North Bedfordshire in 1906, includes the following Midland Road shops (besides the Black Swan public house at no. 33): right from centre, no. 31 Thompson, pawnbroker; no. 29, Armsden, butcher; no. 27, Darlow, gunsmith; no. 25, Nelson, butcher; no. 23, Deacon, confectioner.

From a similar viewpoint in 1977 we see: site of 31 Midland Road, removed to widen Allhallows Lane in the 1920s; no. 29, Kelly's Milk Bar, awaiting demolition along with the Empire Cinema, which had been built on the site of Darlow's in 1912.

The Bedford Co-op at 24–38 Midland Road was an ungainly structure by the 1950s, having absorbed all its neighbours between Gravel Lane (left) and the Golden Lion (right).

The main Co-op was rebuilt in 1970 and its predecessor was replaced by C & A in 1974. The Liberal Club (architects Usher & Anthony 1884) was demolished in 1979; the site is now occupied by Bonmarche and Entertainment Exchange.

On the corner of Gwyn Street, Tom Coombs' Draporium at 57–59 Midland Road (seen here in 1906) remained a draper's shop until Cyril Bates's shop (on the same site) was destroyed by fire in 1964.

Tom Coombs (1857–1916) had another shop at the corner of High Street and The Arcade, which offered goods on credit. Opened in 1906, these premises later became the Cadena Café and are now occupied by Pizza Hut.

Thomas Bates traded at 6–8 St Loyes Street between 1898 and his death in 1914. No. 6 St Loyes Street is still recognisable as The Money Shop, whilst no. 8 (much altered) is now 1st Choice Recruitment.

Harry Hills of 7 Silver Street trained as a draper in London with a contemporary, Austin Reed; the son of each undertook never to open a branch in a town served by the other. These premises later became MacFisheries after Harry Hills (1961) Ltd, a new company, moved to West Arcade, finally closing down in about 1980.

The draper George Hurst (1800–98), mayor of Bedford five times, built 75 High Street in 1851 (the initials G.H. are above the parapet). His shop is best remembered as Dust's, after a later owner, and for the busts of three architects (Palladio, Christopher Wren and Inigo Jones) which adorned the shop-front until demolition in 1957. Laura Ashley is on the site today.

The interior of the first floor of Whitelock, draper and milliner, at 117–119 High Street, *c.* 1920, formerly the premises of Thomas Lester, the lace-dealer. The building was demolished in about 1964 and absorbed into the site of the rebuilt Midland Bank.

J. & A. Beagley had premises at 41 St Peter's Street, shown here, which were demolished for the Merton Centre in 1973. The firm was the main supplier of uniforms for Bedford School.

Welch's, cobbler, at 2 Midland Road, adjoined the north-west boundary of Bedford Modern School and was demolished in about 1962 to provide a bicycle park for the school. William Welch's three shops were all festooned with advertising.

J.H. Boggas, cobbler, 69 Midland Road, stood on the corner of Hassett Street (left) and was demolished in about 1963, together with Macmullen's of Hertford, wine merchants, at no. 67 next door.

Richard Roe's wine and spirit stores and coal depot at 67 Midland Road had an unusual Greek Revival frontage. Latterly occupied by Macmullen's of Hertford, also wine merchants, the premises were demolished in about 1963.

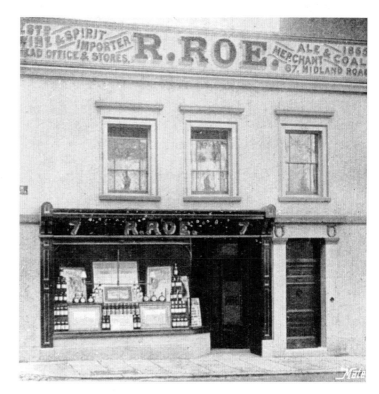

Richard Roe, wine merchant, photographed in 1906, occupied the former home of James Wyatt (1816–78), who founded the *Bedford Times* newspaper in 1845, and kept his archaeological collections in outbuildings stretching back to Lurke Street. Later used as an automobile electrical shop, the building was demolished in 1934 to clear the site for the Granada Cinema.

The works of Samuel Jarvis, monumental mason, at 117 Midland Road, with his residence, Fairfax House, next door; the photograph was taken by his step-son John Moore in September 1960. 117 is now Liberty Hairdressing.

James Perkins at 50 Tavistock Street, seen here in about 1900 with unidentified family members, was an old-established painter and decorator. The shop closed in the 1980s and is now a restaurant.

The bookshop of James Rogers Porter at 5 High Street was photographed by George Downes in 1867. Porter later moved next door to no. 7; the shop in the photograph was formerly occupied by William White (also a printer and bookseller), whose son William Hale White (the novelist Mark Rutherford) was born there in 1831. No. 5 became Beagley's, outfitter (see p. 69 top).

Walter Stanley Bradley, bookseller and stationer, 3 Mill Street, photographed the day after Jack Dempsey (USA) knocked out Luis Firpo of Argentina to retain the world heavyweight boxing championship on 14 September 1923 (the 'big fight result' on the placard). The shop was demolished in the early 1960s, and is the present site of the office entrance at 21–23 Mill Street, following renumbering of properties.

Henry Bacchus, 35 High Street, occupied premises built in 1835 by John Howard the ironfounder, whose prize-winning plough from the Great Exhibition surmounted the parapet from 1851 until 1969. After many years of neglect, this building and its neighbours were converted, appropriately, into a hardware store (Wilkinson's) in 1995.

The interior of Henry Bacchus, *c.* 1903, showing a great profusion of ironmongery, much of which was manufactured in the foundry in Castle Lane at the rear.

The royal Daimler carrying King George V and Queen Mary arrives at W.H. Allen's Queen's Engineering Works (built 1894) at 11.10 a.m. on 27 June 1918.

Workers from W.H. Allen's return home for lunch along Ford End Road in Queen's Park, a suburb built partly to accommodate the workforce. In the foreground is the sign of the Globe public house. On the right is a Gas Company building which was later converted into a showroom.

Workers and foremen at the Higgins Brewery, Castle Lane, March 1895. Built in 1838 by Charles Higgins, landlord of the Swan Hotel, the brewery was sold by his grandson, the connoisseur Cecil Higgins, to Wells & Winch of Biggleswade in 1927. Later occupied by Bennett's Works (clothing factory), then the GPO sorting office, the old brewery was converted into Bedford Museum in 1982.

St Peter's Brewery in Lurke Street was established in 1819, and acquired by F.C. Fuller in the 1880s. The buildings were demolished in 1934 to extend the car park of the newly opened Granada Cinema. Present site of Lidl's car park.

Deacon's, confectioner, at 7 Midland Road, occupied the former residence of James Horsford (1805–86), architect and alderman. The shop closed in 1933 and the site was absorbed by Woolworths.

This old house at 8–10 The Broadway had been one of Dudeney & Johnston's grocer's shops before being taken over by the Bedfordshire Autocar Co., main Ford dealers, in 1919. In about 1932, not long after the date of this photograph, the ceiling collapsed and new buildings were erected on the site (now awaiting redevelopment). Photo 1922.

Texas Instruments Ltd, manufacturers of semi-conductors, made Bedford their UK headquarters in 1957, and built this factory in Dallas Road, off Kempston Road adjoining the railway. The company moved to much larger premises in Manton Lane which were opened in 1963, the original works being converted into industrial units. This photograph was taken on 11 August 1958. Buildings demolished in 2009.

Section Six

CIVIC AMENITIES

This is an interesting 1930s snapshot of the trefoil-decorated cast-iron balustrade of
Prebend Street Bridge (opened in 1884 and replaced in 1992 by County Bridge). On the
left are the Commercial Road baths; in the centre are St Paul's spire and Charles Wells's
brewery chimney; on the right is The Lawns (the Chetham family home).

The Commercial Road swimming baths (opened in 1872), seen here from the Prebend Street end in about 1903, closed in 1957. The island (right) is now a nesting area for waterfowl. The north bank of the river (left) is now called Sovereign's Quay.

The final refurbishment of Newnham Baths in the late 1950s did away with the last remains of Newnham Mill, namely the miller's cottage, seen here in the 1900s. The baths closed in 1980, lay derelict for nine years, and were replaced by the Aspects Leisure Centre.

Bedford General Hospital (architect Percy Adams) was built in 1897 to replace the Bedford Infirmary founded by Samuel Whitbread in 1803. The lime avenue (on the right) leading from Kempston Road to the infirmary was blocked by the new hospital chapel (demolished in 1978). Some of the trees still survive.

The Victoria Ward (for children) in the new hospital is decorated with twenty ceramic representations of fairy tales and nursery rhymes designed by Philip Newman and executed by W.B. Simpson & Sons. The cost was met by sixteen local ladies – whose names are recorded over the entrance (right) – to commemorate Queen Victoria's Diamond Jubilee in 1897. Now used as the stroke recovery ward.

The Convent School at 112–114 Bromham Road was built in 1889 as Crescent House Ladies' College, and sold to the Daughters of the Holy Ghost in 1914. The Convent School closed in July 1974, and the buildings were used by St Bede's RC Middle School, until it closed in 2006.

The gymnasium of Crescent House Ladies' College, with the instructor, Sergeant-Major Penn, *c.* 1903. This building adjoined the main school on the west side, and was replaced by the Convent School hall and classroom block in 1929.

The exterior of the Physical Education College gymnasium in Lansdowne Road, built in about 1920 and replaced by a dance-drama hall (now the Bowen-West Theatre) in 1965. The PE College was founded by Margaret Stansfeld in 1903. The Bowen-West Theatre closed in 2006.

Although taken in the early 1930s, this picture of PE College students with young children could date from twenty years later, when the present author was amongst pupils of Polam School (then in Chaucer Road), whose PE lessons took place in Lansdowne Road.

The General Post Office in Dame Alice Street was built in stages from 1896. Replaced by the new head post office in Dane Street in 1975, this building then became the Central Club (successor to the Liberal Club in Midland Road) with an entrance in Harpur Street.

The coffee tavern on the corner of Harpur Street (left) and Silver Street, *c.* 1880. The brick building with chimney (right) was the borough police station. Boots rebuilt the corner site in 1896 (it is now Clinton Cards).

CHURCH AND CHAPEL

This is the earliest known topographical sketch of Bedford, and shows John Bunyan (1628–88) preaching

outside the Guildhall on the corner of High Street and St Paul's Square (north side). It is also the only

picture of the Guildhall, which was demolished after 1803. On the left are the Swan Inn and the gatehouse

on the old Town Bridge. In the original engraving, the image is reversed.

Holy Trinity Church (1840, architect John Brown of Norwich), was photographed by George Downes before the chancel was added in 1865. The tower pinnacles were removed in 1927. On the far right are the entrance gates to the 'Best' Almshouses on Harpur Green, with the westernmost almshouse visible behind. (This was the future site of Bedford High School.)

The interior of Holy Trinity Church in 1974, showing the galleries and chancel arch. All the fittings were removed in 1980, and a new floor was inserted at gallery level, during conversion of the church into a dining hall (ground floor) and classrooms (first floor) for the High School.

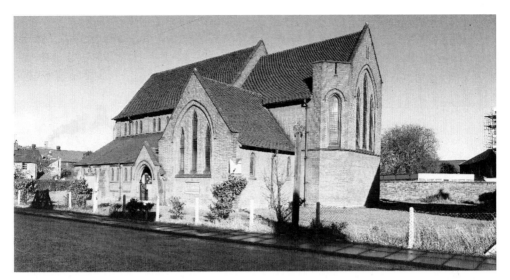

St Leonard's Church in Victoria Road was built in 1911 (architect G.P. Allen) to replace a tin church founded by the Rev. Paul Wyatt in 1889. The west end (left) was never completed. The south transept containing the Wyatt Memorial Chapel stands nearest the camera.

Looking to the west end from the chancel arch of St Leonard's in 1974, with the Wyatt Chapel (left), which commemorates Paul Wyatt's parents James (who founded the *Bedford Times* in 1845) and Augusta. Declared redundant in 1974, the church was later used as workshops by the Manpower Services Commission. It was damaged by fire in 1988 and demolished in 1990. The Wyatt memorial tablets have been preserved.

The graveyard of Bunyan Meeting, *c.* 1890, with William Rogers, the chapel keeper, standing by the tomb of the Rev. Samuel Hillyard, pastor from 1790 to 1839. Behind is the rear wall of Howard House. Most of the gravestones were thrown down in 1928, as paving for the John Bunyan memorial garden in the tercentenary year of his birth.

A sketch of the interior of the Old Meeting (built in 1707), looking north (towards Mill Street) after 1838, when gas-lighting was installed. The building could seat about seven hundred and was full every Sunday. Communicant members of the church sat in the box pews, the rest of the congregation filling the galleries. All stood with their backs to the minister during prayers of up to thirty-five minutes in length.

Bunyan Meeting, seen here *c*. 1890, was built in 1849–50 (architects J.T. Wing and T.J. Jackson) to replace the Old Meeting of 1707, itself standing on the site of a barn where John Bunyan had preached. The front wall was set back for road-widening in about 1960, minus the superb 'overthrow' lamp.

The interior of Bunyan Meeting, *c*. 1900, showing the side galleries and some of the pews (removed in 1974). The galleries are now linked across the front of the organ, and the stencil decorations have been painted over.

Howard House, 55 Mill Street, was the town house of John Howard the philanthropist (1726–90) when he was a member of the Old Meeting, whose congregation he left to become the principal benefactor of the New Meeting (later Howard Congregational Church), built in 1774.

Howard House was acquired in 1883 as the home of the Bunyan Institute (a club for church members) and of the chapel keeper. The northernmost bay was removed to widen the corner with Mill Street in about 1960. On the right are the former Fire Station (1888) and 38 Mill Street (1760). Howard House was renovated in 1995.

The Baptist Church in Mill Street was designed by John Usher, and opened in 1864 on the site of an earlier chapel deriving from a secession from the Old (now Bunyan) Meeting. In his drawing F.T. Mercer has omitted the shops which adjoined the church on both sides, and were demolished along with it in 1964.

The Salvation Army Citadel, photographed in 1977 shortly before demolition and replacement by the Howard (shopping) Centre multi-storey car-park. The architect of the citadel was G.G. Wallace of Northampton. The large hall (right) could seat 1,100.

General William Booth (1829–1912), founder of the Salvation Army, seen here on a visit to Bedford *c.* 1908. He had laid the keystone of the entrance to the citadel in River Street on 3 October 1888.

Section Eight

SOME PEOPLE

Attending the foundation stone laying of Pearcey Road (now Shackleton Lower) School

on 28 July 1927 are the mayor, Gilbert Barford, with (from left on platform) the

mayor's sergeant, Alderman Hockliffe, Walter Laughton (the builder),

G.P. Allen (the architect), S.C. George (education committee secretary), the

Rev. G.G. Brown, rector of St Mary's. The school would accommodate 350 children

and cost £14,000.

A game of croquet in the garden of Howard House before the building of the present Bunyan Museum in 1891. On the far right is William Rogers the chapel keeper. In the background are the trees in the garden of Castle Close (see p. 85, bottom).

The High Street grocer W.H. Elliott (with watch-chain) and Alderman Gilbert Barford at the Priory Street bowling green, c. 1920. The tall building on the left is Holy Trinity Sunday Schoolroom in Roise Street. The recreation ground swings (see p. 10, bottom) are also visible.

The builders of St Leonard's Church in Victoria Road, photographed as the church nears completion in 1913. The Wyatt Chapel is awaiting its roof-tiles.

The builders of the council houses in Mile Road, Bedford, *c*. 1919–20. The young man wearing a military blouse (far right, second row from the front) is Edwin Peacock.

William Thomas Baker, bookseller, stationer, printer and sub-postmaster, outside 12 St Mary's Street during the Bedford Shopping Carnival, 1–9 October 1920. His son, Jack Baker (1917–99), was the third generation owner of this family business, founded on the opposite side of the street in 1869, and situated at the above address since 1880. It is now a Post Office and Londis store.

HIGH STREET

Looking north from the Town Bridge, c. 1905, with the George Inn on the right. This was once an important coaching inn, from whose prominent first-floor bay window the arrival and departure of stage coaches could be observed.

George Gearey took this photograph in 1938, shortly before the demolition of Bank Buildings (left) to widen the Town Bridge. On the right is Murkett's car-showroom, formerly the George Inn.

The east side of the High Street, *c.* 1900, with the George Inn (right) and adjoining it, no. 5 (with lamp), the birthplace of Mark Rutherford (1831–1913).

Murkett's (formerly the George Inn) was demolished in 1959, to be followed by nos 5 (Beagley's) and 7 (Hague, sports shop). They were all replaced by the Swan Court development.

John Bull, goldsmiths and watch and clock merchants, first opened in 1817, and rebuilt 47–49 High Street in 1878. The business moved to St Peter's Street in 1964, at which time the superb late Victorian shop-front (seen here in 1906) was destroyed.

Here are 65–69 High Street in the mid-1890s, with R. Willshaw's music warehouse at no. 65 (right) and G. Shaw (jeweller and optician) at no. 67. These premises are now the Showboat amusement arcade. On the left is the Cross Keys public house, at no. 69, which closed in 2009.

This photograph of the junction of High Street with Mill Street (left) and Silver Street (right) dates from the 1880s. Draper's (right) at 56 High Street was once the Crown Inn, and was demolished to widen the corner in 1937. E.P. Rose (now Debenhams) rebuilt much of the west side of High Street at this point. Elliott's, grocer (left), was replaced by the former Prudential building in 1938. Then comes the Cross Keys.

Jelley & Clarke at 73 High Street, seen here in 1906, was an old-established grocer's shop, later sold to Grimbly Hughes. 'Why the Dickins does Amies throw Dust on Clarke's Jelleys?' was a conundrum containing the names of several adjacent High Street shops.

Grimbly Hughes, successor to Jelley & Clarke in about 1930, awaits demolition, c. 1957, to be replaced by Alexandre, outfitter; this in turn became the AA in 1983. It is now a kitchen/bedroom/bathroom store. Dust's at no. 75 (see p. 38) is on the left.

This block of shops with dwellings above (now renumbered 95–105 High Street) was built by George Handscombe Miller in the early 1860s and was photographed by George Downes in about 1869. Some of the Ionic columns on the ground floor may still be seen. To the right is part of Miss Langley's garden wall (the future site of more shops).

The opposite (west) side of High Street, *c.* 1926, from Watford's, wine merchant, at no. 76 (now Jessop, photo centre). Hockliffe's bookshop, with awning lowered, is prominent in the background.

In 1887, 107 High Street was occupied by Mrs Ellen Sim's wool and fancy warehouse. By 1894 it was Day & Son, ironmongers, which became Golding & Grant (founded in 1867) soon after 1897. Here is Goldings in 1906, now the longest surviving High Street business, still trading as general ironmongers.

Barclays Bank took over Tansley's, butchers at 111 High Street in about 1920, and rebuilt the premises (taking in the site of no. 109, which was occupied by Mrs Susannah Ham, china dealer) in 1929. This photograph dates from about 1920.

Rose's pianoforte and music warehouse at 123 High Street occupied the St Peter's Street corner of Duke's Row, a terrace of two-storey dwellings (built *c.* 1800) of which this (now a newsagent and a restaurant) is the only survivor. Duke's Row originally extended as far as Lurke Street.

Dudeney & Johnston, grocers, built this large shop at 100 High Street in about 1900, on the corner of Dame Alice Street (right). The upper floor housed their Indian Tea Rooms. In the post-war period, these premises became Weatherhead's (electrical goods), whose record department was upstairs. The building lately Porter Black's, is now empty.

Section Ten

ENTERTAINMENT

The building of the roller skating rink along The Embankment adjoining the Town and County Club in 1910 marked the beginning of the era of indoor mass entertainment in Bedford. The rink was also available for political meetings: Lloyd George spoke here in favour of free trade soon after it was opened.

With the end of the roller-skating craze, the rink was divided in two in 1920, the western half becoming the Café Dansant and the eastern half Murkett's Garage. The Plaza Cinema replaced the Café Dansant in 1929, and Bedford Museum was established in the old Murkett's in 1962. Cinema and museum were demolished in 1981–2.

The County Theatre in Midland Road was built as an auction room in 1891 and opened as a theatre by Edward Graham-Falcon on 1 April 1899. The iron-and-glass canopy was destroyed by bomb-blast in 1942, and the façade was refronted in about 1957.

The interior of the County Theatre, with the stage set for *The Barretts of Wimpole Street* by Rudolf Besier, starring Wilfrid Lawson as Edward Barrett, in February 1949. The theatre was sold by auction that year following the death of Graham-Falcon. All the Victorian decor was removed in 1957 as part of a modernisation scheme, but the theatre closed in 1960, and was used as a bingo club until 1995. It is now a church.

Robert Chetham went into the cinema business and leased the Picturedrome, Bedford's first purpose-built cinema (opened in 1910, demolished in 1964) from the Blake brothers. He later developed the Plaza Cinema (see p. 76) from part of the old rink.

Mate's Illustrated Guide to Bedford (1906) records that weekly band concerts were held on the River Ouse or along The Embankment during the summer, and this photograph is evidence of their great popularity.

Spectators crowd both banks of the Ouse during the Regatta, 25 July 1912. This photograph, by Blake & Edgar, looks upstream from near the suspension bridge.

The boat-slide at the weir opposite Russell Park enabled the hirers of punts and skiffs to transfer from the upper River Ouse (seen here) to the lower river and vice versa. It has been derelict for many years. This photograph and the one on p. 82 were taken by Ferdy Richards in about 1906.

A view of part of Boat Slide Weir bridge (opened in 1896) from the lower river. The rustic balustrading was replaced in the 1970s.

Section Eleven

MANY MANSIONS

Old Gaston House on the corner of Lurke Street and St Cuthbert's Street (right) had its exterior remodelled by Albert Prosser, c. 1920. When previously owned by Carl St Amory, it was the intended site of his Bedford Opera House. The house was restored as offices in the late 1970s. It is now a dental practice.

St Mary's Abbey, a private house at 32 Cardington Road, had rear extensions said to incorporate stones from the church of St Peter de Dunstable (demolished 1545) and the Chapel of Herne in St Paul's Square (demolished 1812). Later an hotel and then the dining hall of Dame Alice Harpur School, the Abbey was demolished in 1969 and replaced by Harpur House almshouses.

The Moravian businessman Charles Trapp built a group of three stone *cottages ornés* along Bromham Road in the 1850s, of which this is the semi-detached pair, nos 126–128. Derelict by the early 1970s, the pair was restored by the Bradley family in about 1980, when the 1950s garage extension at no. 126 was removed.

This curious timber-framed house, photographed in September 1913 shortly before demolition, was 124 Bromham Road, another part of Trapp's development. It backed on to a market-garden which later became the site of the Territorial Army drill-hall.

Castle Close, seen here in about 1943, was built in 1846 by Charles Higgins next door to his Castle Lane brewery (see p. 46). It was the childhood home of his grandson, the connoisseur Cecil Higgins, who sold it in 1910. Acquired by Bedford Corporation in 1924, it has housed the Cecil Higgins Art Gallery since 1949. A large extension was built to the left of the Victorian mansion in 1973.

These houses on the east side of Ashburnham Road (renumbered since the photograph was taken, *c.* 1905) are (from right) West Wick (no. 95), Woodleigh (no. 97) and Fairfield (no. 99, formerly Red Cross House). West Wick was a High School boarding house in the 1880s.

The back garden of Woodleigh (97 Ashburnham Road), residence of the Rev. Charles ('Tinker') Hemsley, a Bedford Modern School master from 1880 to 1913 who also took in school boarders. The photographer was Alfred Burns, school secretary from 1879 to 1932.

Another of Burns's colleagues was the Rev. H.W. ('Tubby') Evans, seen here at Glanfraed, 9 Dynevor Road, *c.* 1905. He also accepted school boarders. His daughter Molly was one of the first students at the PE College in nearby Lansdowne Road. She taught gymnastics, soccer and woodwork at Bedford Modern, and as secretary of Polam Preparatory School in the early 1950s took classes which included the present author. Glanfraed is now a nursing home.

Glanyrafon, 1 Newnham Road, was built in 1883 by William Seys Phillips, mathematics master at the Grammar School, as a school boarding house. Later renamed Kirkman's, it was demolished in 1968 to extend the Christie Almshouses.

At the north-east corner of Union Street is no. 69 (left, seen here *c.* 1910), the residence for many years of Walter Joseph Meller, engineer, and his daughter Gertrude, a music teacher. The house, which they called Red Craig, is now the Italian Cultural Centre.

This photograph of 19 Rothsay Road, adjacent to the Castle Road roundabout, was reproduced on a postcard postmarked 1 September 1908, when the householder was Frederick Fuller. The house looks virtually the same today.

Bushmead Avenue, seen here looking south in 1906, is one of Bedford's spacious late Victorian residential streets. It was named after Bushmead Priory, the north Bedfordshire seat of the Wade-Gery family who once owned the land.

De Parys Avenue, here looking south, c. 1910, is Bedford's finest residential street, laid out from the early 1880s. At far left is no. 67, Kirkman's boarding house for Bedford School from 1968 to 1993. The Attenborough mansion, at no. 58, is on the far right.

Holbrook, 58 De Parys Avenue, when it was the residence of Walter Attenborough, Conservative MP for Bedford between the two general elections of 1910. Built in about 1890 as Aira Holm for Arthur Sutherland, it was by far the biggest private house in the town.

The site of Holbrook occupied the entire corner block of De Parys Avenue and Park Avenue. The property was sold for redevelopment in about 1936 and replaced by five houses (even nos 58–66) in De Parys Avenue and six houses (continuous nos 5–10) in Park Avenue. Part of the garden wall survives on the corner of the two roads.

The architect Albert Prosser (1870–1961) built 14 Park Avenue for his family in about 1925, with his single-storey office on the corner of De Parys Avenue next to a further house for sale (far right). The site had previously been a paddock.

No. 19 Goldington Road was built after 1856, but Albert Prosser remodelled the entrance in about 1910, as seen here. The house later became the Christian Science reading room and was demolished in about 1965.

This pair of houses, 90 and 92 Kimbolton Road, was built by Albert Prosser in about 1905, in what was then a country road. The family lived at no. 90 (left) before moving to Old Gaston House in St Cuthbert's Street (see p. 83).

The ingenious use of the chimney-stack as an architectural feature marks out 1 Devon Road as a characteristic Prosser design.

Section Twelve

HUMBLE HOMES

*At the time of this 1950s photograph, 1–3 Peel Street were used by J.P. Simmons & Sons
(furniture shop), round the corner in Tavistock Street. The workshop of Charles Negus Ltd
(right of sign) is today the only survivor (now the Dragon Inn).*

Thomas Christie's almshouses in St Loyes Street were built in 1682 on part of the site of Allhallows Church, acquired by the Christie family after the Reformation. Eight poor widows were provided with a cottage and a small income, the rest of the endowment going to support the fabric and incumbent of St Paul's Church. The photograph dates from May 1961.

The Christie Almshouses await demolition in 1961, to be replaced by new almshouses on the corner of The Embankment and Newnham Road. The former cycle shop at 64 St Loyes Street is now Wilson Peacock, estate agents.

The Harpur Trust built the 'Six-and-Forty' almshouses in Dame Alice Street between 1801 and 1816, originally as cottages for rent, and refronted them in the 1880s. The eastern half, seen here in the 1920s, was modernised internally in the mid-1960s, and the western half was demolished in 1969. Sold to private owners in 2000.

Nos 49–59 Union Street (photographed in 1977) dated from the early nineteenth century and were demolished for an extension (which was never built) to the Tavistock Health Centre. No. 49 (far right) had been Mrs Lilian Summerfield's shop; she was a newsagent and tobacconist. The site is now a car park.

Beauchamp Row, romantically named after the barons of Bedford Castle, was a group of cottages built north of the Friary Farm in the 1830s.

Beauchamp Court, which had replaced Beauchamp Row by about 1960, appears in the background. In the centre is the Lord John public house at 104–106 Greyfriars Walk, on the corner of Roise Street, with Roise Court under construction (foreground).

View of the future site of the bus station, with the backs of houses in Allhallows Lane (centre), and (right) properties in Thurlow Street. The back of the Pentecostal Church in Gwyn Street is in the left foreground.

'Weird Wellsian Monsters' was a contemporary newspaper description of the tower-blocks in the central area redevelopment. At one time the Pentecostal Church at 44–46 Gwyn Street (centre) stood isolated on the bus station forecourt. In the background is Beckett Court under construction.

Nos 41–45 Cauldwell Street await demolition in about 1968, their site to become part of the County Hall car park. Beyond the hoardings (right) is the Mander College teaching block, which replaced St Mary's Wesleyan Church.

A pre-1914 photograph of floods in Cauldwell Street, with clothier C.W. Campling (right) at no. 52. On the corner of Farrer Street is A.C. Boone, printer (centre). The right-hand premises later became Bob King, motorcycles, the site now being occupied by The Horseshoe (flats).

Section Thirteen

ROYAL OCCASIONS

King George V and Queen Mary leave the High School after their visit on 27 June 1918,
which lasted half an hour. Former pupils in Voluntary Aid Detachment nursing uniforms
stand on the left. Nearest the King is Miss Dolby, headmistress of the Girls' Modern
School, with Miss Collie, headmistress of the High School, looking on.

The southern part of High Street, decorated for the coronation of King Edward VII on 9 August 1902. On the left is the Cross Keys public house; on the right is E.P. Rose, draper, later rebuilt, now Debenhams.

Children's party to celebrate the coronation in 1911, held in Bedford (Grammar) School's playing-field, with the pavilion (built in 1899, rebuilt in 1934) in the background.

The northern end of High Street, decorated for the coronation of King George V on 22 June 1911. Westminster Bank is to the right: F. Gamman, house furnisher, at no. 85, later Superdrug, is in the centre. The photographer was J. Schrader, who lived at 6 Gibbons Road.

Harpur Street, looking south from the corner of St Loyes Street (right), with Silver Jubilee decorations, 1935.

The north side of St Paul's Square, decorated for the Silver Jubilee of King George V in 1935. All the buildings still stand, except Mayes (corn and seed merchant), west of the Corn Exchange (centre).

Silver Jubilee decorations in St Cuthbert's Street. The garden wall on the corner of Grove Place (right) was demolished in about 1970, thereby removing the sense of enclosure at this point in the street scene.

The Queen visits the Bunyan (sports) Centre, 11 May 1976. Immediately to the right of Her Majesty are Councillor Ken Scott and Mrs Dorothy Wildman. Councillor George Newman is in the wheelchair, with Councillor Paul Hooley standing behind him. Next right are Councillor Edgar Valentine, Mrs Hooley and Mrs Valentine.

Section Fourteen

VANISHED PUBS

The Boot Inn, 20–22 Midland Road, stood on the corner of Gravel Lane (right), before demolition in 1912 and replacement by the Bedford Co-op. This is the present site of New Look (fashion store).

Pencil drawing (1898) by A.G. Glass of the White Horse public house in Midland Road, also showing the west side of Harpur Street (right) in considerable detail. Note the Star public house, with a horizontally projecting lantern, and the Albion public house (far right), also with a lantern. The White Horse was replaced by Marks & Spencer in 1929.

This snapshot of Harpur Street in about 1938 shows the Star, rebuilt in the early 1930s to a new building line (left). It was absorbed into the Marks & Spencer site in the early 1960s. Beyond Canvin, butcher, soon to be rebuilt, is the Albion public house.

Looking south down Harpur Street in August 1938 we see the Albion, just before it was replaced by the new Canvin's (now the site of Mothercare). Dynes, fruiterer, site of the Woolwich Building now Barclays, is on the far right. The small kiosk-like structure is part of the Ideal Home Bureau hardware shop.

This is the yard of the Albion (left) in September 1923, present site of West Arcade. The central building, formerly stables, was converted into the Ideal Home Bureau in about 1925.

The Roise Street corner of the Lord John public house in Greyfriars Walk, with Roise Court under construction, *c.* 1960. Lord John Russell failed by one vote to become MP for Bedford in 1830. The name of Roise Street has been transferred to the surviving north end of Greyfriars Walk.

The Golden Lion, 40 Midland Road, seen here with the landlord Harry Lawson in the mid-1920s, stood on the corner of River Street (right). He had been landlord since 1906, when he moved from the Black Swan at 33 Midland Road. The Golden Lion was demolished to widen River Street in the early 1970s.

The Coach and Horses in Prebend Street (part of which was then called Cauldwell Road) was built in 1896 to replace a public house of the same name in St Paul's Square, where public lavatories stood until 2004. On the left is the chimney of the Electricity Works. The pub closed in the 1980s and is now empty.

THE RIVERSIDE

The steam launch Lady Lena plied the river (together with the Lodore and Lorna Doone)

every summer from the 1890s, using the steps near the Swan Hotel as a landing stage.

The Chetham family of boat-builders had their repair yard at Batts Ford, seen here in the 1920s. To the right of the trees are the slipper baths (public washrooms). The new Salvation Army Citadel now stands on the right-hand site.

The aftermath of the fire at Hobson's timber-yard, upstream from the Town Bridge, 21 June 1917. These buildings had been part of Nash's Brewery until about 1890, and this site was to become part of St Mary's Embankment in 1923.

The principal boat-hiring station was situated just downstream from the Town Bridge, opposite the Swan Hotel (right). Also prominent in this photograph of 1896 are Bank Buildings (centre) and the George Inn (next to the Swan).

The same (north) bank of the river, *c.* 1882, this time looking west, before the balustrading was erected along The Embankment. The roadway occupied the site of the Swan Hotel gardens.

The Ouse in spate during 1918. The elegant Town Bridge (architect John Wing) was opened in 1813, but was not made free of toll until 1 July 1835, during the mayoralty of Dr George Witt, who lived at St Mary's Abbey (see p. 84, top).

Looking downstream from the Swan Hotel during the same or a similar period of flooding. Duck Mill Weir Bridge is in the background (right).

The balustrading can be seen in this flood photograph, perhaps taken in 1918. On the right is the east end of the roller-skating rink of 1910, later the home of Bedford Museum.

Boats for hire along The Embankment, 1920s. The boatman also looked after customers' bicycles. On the right are Mill Meadows, opened as a recreation ground in 1888.

The only public house to be permitted along The Embankment was the Embankment Hotel, built by Higgins' Brewery in 1891, and pictured here in a drawing by A.G. Glass. Opposite, the surviving cottages of 'Waterloo' await demolition (this is the site of the Embankment Gardens).

The Embankment promenade, photographed by Ferdy Richards, *c.* 1906. On the left is Billy Keech, and next to him John Hamson, assistant editor of the *Bedfordshire Times*.

Further downstream, there was extensive tree cover, with willows planted by Dr Jabez Carter in the 1880s prominent on the river bank. These survived into the 1960s.

The Embankment Gardens with their coloured lights strung along through the trees, seen here in an Edwardian postcard view, were the creation of Norman Greenshields, borough surveyor from 1901 to 1932.

The Promenade, Bedford

Another Edwardian postcard view of the Promenade, *c.* 1910. The girl on the left (centre foreground) is Elsie Crawley, later Mrs Rump, who died in the early 1980s.

The Suspension Bridge, seen here from Mill Meadows, *c.* 1900, was designed by John J. Webster and opened by the Marquess of Tavistock on 11 July 1888. It became a listed building in 1995.

This photograph shows snow clearing near the foot of the Suspension Bridge after the great snowstorm on 24 April 1908.

An early victim of the scrap-metal drive in the Second World War was the Russian ship cannon, a Crimean War trophy seen here on its concrete plinth (which still survives) south of Russell Park.

At the extreme eastern end of The Embankment was the rustic Newnham Bridge, a favourite resort of courting couples in the nineteenth century. It was swept away in a flood in 1936 and replaced by the present concrete footbridge.

Section Sixteen

OUTSKIRTS

*Looking south down Barkers Lane, Goldington, early 1900s. The pair of houses (centre)
and adjoining terrace (right) still stand. Goldington parish was absorbed into the
borough of Bedford in 1934.*

The Lodge, Clapham Road, which stood in extensive grounds in the angle of Clapham Road and Manton Lane, was built by the Fitzpatrick family in about 1850, and was last lived in by Robert Elgie, Clerk of the Harpur Trust, who died in 1964. The house was then demolished and the site is now occupied by the Sports Hall of Bedford Modern School.

The weekend retreat of the ironmonger Frederic Gale (now 48 Putnoe Lane) looking south-east across Laxton's Nursery, c. 1920. The scent of Laxton's roses so irritated his breathing that the house was later given up.

The Kimbolton Road lodge of Clapham Park, designed by John Usher in 1877. The driveway is now a public pathway along Falcon Avenue, and the lodge is a private house.

Clapham Park was the country seat of James Howard (1821–89), Liberal MP for Bedford and co-founder of Britannia Ironworks. Sold after his death, the house was later bought back by the family; subsequent owners were Manor House Hospital (Golders Green) and the Daughters of the Holy Ghost, who ran the Convent School in Bromham Road (see p. 52, top) and who sold Clapham Park in 1986 to developers for conversion into flats.

Provender Farm (also known as Davey's Farm) stood west of the Midland Railway line, on the future site of Hurst Grove. Seen here are Charles Davey and his family in about 1880.

Prebend Farm also stood west of the railway, but further south, where Coventry Road now joins Ford End Road. It too was tenanted by members of the Davey family.

Austin Canons was built on the Bedford-Kempston boundary by the Rev. Paul Wyatt in 1891, to a joint design by himself and Henry Young. The north wing (left) was added in 1895 for his mother Augusta (widow of James Wyatt of the *Bedford Times*). She appears in the photograph, dressed in black. Sold by the Wyatt family in 1940, Austin Canons was twice converted into flats, most recently in 1992, when the north wing was demolished. Austin Canons was demolished in 2000.

This horse-trough, photographed in 1977, stood in Kempston Road just west of the railway bridge, and according to the plaque was presented to the borough by 'Amelia, widow of J.B.', in April 1895. Subject to frequent damage by traffic, the trough, which incorporates a drinking bowl for dogs on the left-hand side of the plinth, was removed to the courtyard of Bedford Museum in the 1980s.

Acknowledgements

The author and publishers are grateful to the county archivist, Christopher Pickford, for permission to reproduce photographs in this book from collections held at the Bedfordshire Record Office at County Hall in Bedford. Most of the prints were made (and in some cases the photographs were taken) over many years by Ken Whitbread and Dave Stubbs of Bedfordshire County Council's photographic service. Numerous lenders have contributed photographs or permitted copies to be made, and particular thanks are due to the following (with apologies for any inadvertent omissions):

Mike Allen • Col. Anstee • the late Donald Armstrong • Bedford Museum
the *Bedfordshire Times* (together with its staff photographers and entrants to its heritage photographic competition in 1977) • the late Mrs P.E. Bickerdike
Mr Blackburn • Mrs B. Blythe • H.S. Bradley • Miss H. Brough
Mrs B.M. Bryant • Bunyan Meeting • Alan Campbell • Mrs G. Candlin
Mrs R.W. Carman • Andrew Clark • Mrs D. Clark • Miss Coleman
conservation section, Bedfordshire County Council planning department
Miss Joan Corfield • Mr and Mrs E.W. Curtis • Mr and Mrs A. Dakin
J. Davey • Mr Deacon • Mrs E. Dunn • the late A.G. East • D.F. Eaton
Mr Edwards • Gerry Finding • Miss S.M. Frost • the late Ronald Gale
W.H.J. Garrard • the late Bob Geary • John Gedge • Richard Hutchins
E.G. Keightley • Mrs R. Marks • Marks & Spencer • Mrs H. Miller
the late John Moore • Mr Nutting • John Payne • the late Miss Barbara Peacock
Dudley Peacock • Edwin Peacock • R.A. Pestell • Mrs Preedy • C. Prigmore
the late Miss Ruby Prosser • Mrs E. Rawlinson • Mrs R.A. Rayner • Frank Richards
Terry Rooke • Keith Rose • John Smith • Miss P.M. Smith • G. Sparks
Miss B.B. Thompson • the late Mrs Diana Tompkins • John Wainwright
Miss Watson • Charles Wells • Miss Ann Whiffin • Miss L. Whiting • Tom Windsor
J. Whyley • John and Joan Wyatt.

The author would also like to thank those who kindly supplied information about photographs and generally helped in the compilation of this book:

the staff of Bedfordshire Record Office • Jack Baker • Sue Banks
Graham Bates • Patricia Bell • Alan Cirket • James Collett-White
Alan Crawley • Alan Edwards • Rosemary Harris • Nigel Lutt • Joyce Negus
Dorothy Richardson • Andrew Underwood • Dorothy Wildman
and Sylvia Woods.

The back issues of the *Bedfordshire Magazine* (1947 to date), *A Bedfordshire Bibliography* by L.R. Conisbee, *The Story of Bedford* by Joyce Godber, and *Bunyan Meeting, Bedford 1650–1950* by H.G. Tibbutt have also proved invaluable, as has the work of generations of anonymous compilers of Bedford street directories from the 1860s to 1976.